29

COLLABORATIONS:
ENGLISH IN OUR LIVES

BEGINNING 1 STUDENT BOOK

The publication of *Collaborations* was directed by the members of the Heinle & Heinle Secondary and Adult ESL Publishing Team:

Publisher: Stanley Galek
Editorial Director: Roseanne Mendoza
Production Services Coordinator: Lisa McLaughlin
Market Development Director: Elaine Uzan Leary

Also participating in the publication of the program were:

Director of Production: Elizabeth Holthaus
Assistant Editor: Ann Keefe
Manufacturing Coordinator: Mary Beth Hennebury
Full Service Design and Production: PC&F, Inc.
Illustration Program: Brian Karas and PC&F, Inc.

Manufactured in the United States of America.

ISBN: 0-8384-4106-8

Heinle & Heinle is a division of International Thomson Publishing, Inc.

Photo Credits
Cover: Julie Graber, top; Jann Huizenga, center left; Bettmann Archive, center middle; Nancy Hunter Warren, center right; Mark Neyndorff, bottom.
Unit 1: FPG, 1; Mark Neyndorff, 2, 3, 12, 13; Jann Huizenga, 8, 9, 15 bottom left; Maria Thomas-Ruzic, 8 bottom left; Helen Gittings, 15 top right, 16.
Unit 2: FPG, 19; Sarah Hoskins, 20, 24, 25, 27, 28; Peter Stazione, 25 top left, 25 top right; Anna Henderson, 29; Jann Huizenga, 30, 33 right; Nikos Nafpliotis, 32; Ziqiang Shr, 33 left.
Unit 3: James Higgins, 35, 36, 44, 45; Nancy Hunter Warren, 40 top; Ziqiang Shr, 40 bottom, 43, 46 right; Bettmann Archive, 41 top; Julie Graber, 41 bottom; Jann Huizenga, 46 left.
Unit 4: Nancy Hunter Warren, 49; Jann Huizenga, 50, 56, 58; Ken Light, 54, 55; James Higgins, 57; Ann Savino, 59; Nikos Nafpliotis, 60 top; Calvin Wharton, 60 bottom.
Unit 5: FPG, 65; Jann Huizenga, 66, 68, 70, 71, 73; Alan Malschick, 74, 75, 77; Betty Lynch, 76.
Unit 6: Marcus Tate, 79; Peter Lee, 80, 91; San Francisco Convention and Visitors Bureau, 86 top left; Jann Huizenga, 86 top right; James Higgins, 86 bottom right, 92 left; Nancy Hunter Warren, 86 bottom left, 87 left; Kitty Leaken, 87 top right; Julie Graber, 87 bottom right; Steve Northup, 90; Calvin Wharton, 92 right; Ziqiang Shr, 93.

COLLABORATIONS:
ENGLISH IN OUR LIVES

BEGINNING 1 STUDENT BOOK

Jann Huizenga
Gail Weinstein-Shr

Heinle & Heinle Publishers
A Division of International Thomson Publishing, Inc.
Boston, MA 02116, U.S.A.

I(T)P   The ITP logo is a trademark under license.

CONTENTS

Language Structures	Higher Order Skills and Strategies	Community Building in the Classroom
• *be* • singular / plural nouns • *like* + infinitive • question formation	• guessing meaning from context • making generalizations • comparing • focused listening • solving problems • evaluating learning	• mapping where we are from • making a class background chart • making a bulletin board display about our countries
• adverbs of frequency • *like* + infinitive • question formation	• making inferences • thinking about learning • focused listening • evaluating learning	• getting help from classmates • sharing ways we like to learn
• *in* and *on* with place names • future with *going to* • *have* • *Wh* questions	• comparing • focused listening • evaluating learning	• learning about one another's families • sharing family photos
• simple present • *can* + verb • *at / from . . . to* with time phrases	• comparing • evaluating • focused listening • putting events in chronological order • evaluating learning	• sharing daily schedules • demonstrating skills and hobbies
• present continuous • compound sentences with *and* or *but*	• categorizing • focused listening • analyzing • evaluating learning	• sharing favorite ways to meet people and make friends
• simple past • future with *going to* • *in* and *on* with dates	• focused listening • planning and organizing an event • comparing • evaluating learning	• sharing photos and information on favorite celebrations • planning a class celebration • making a class calendar

THE WORLD

Do you want to see where the people in this book come from? Their countries are labeled.

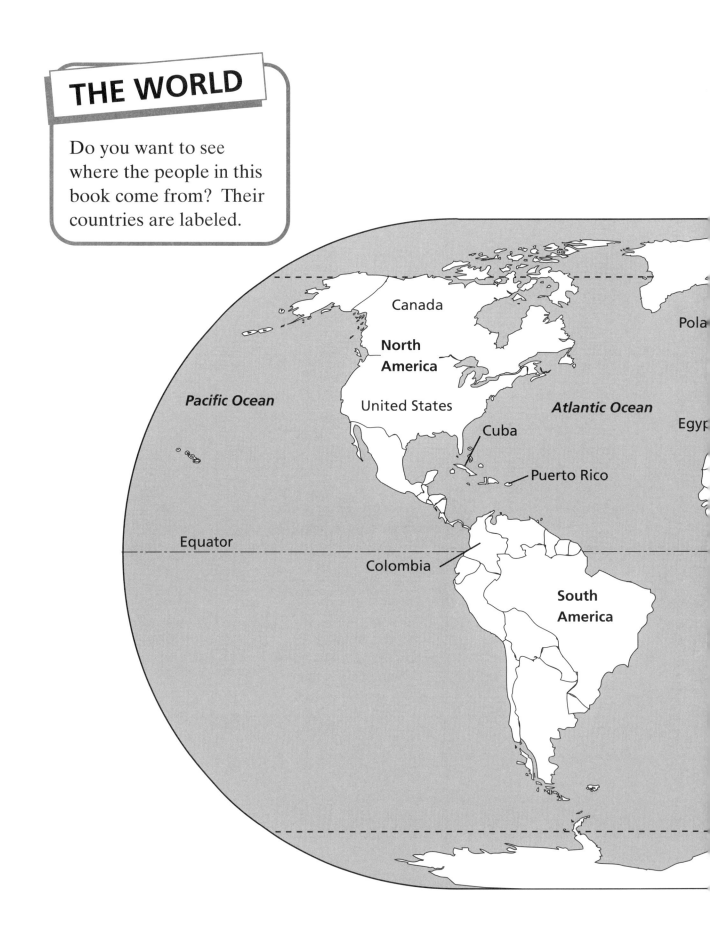

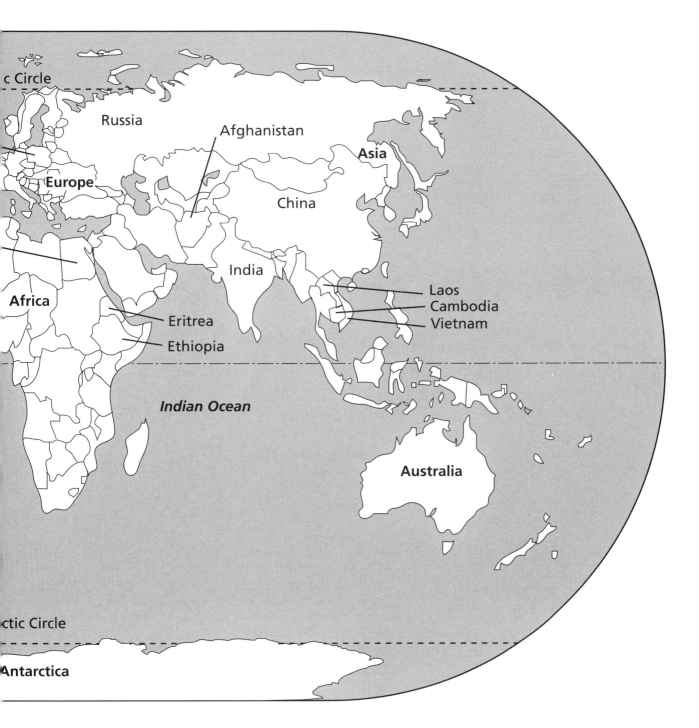

c Circle

Russia

Afghanistan

Asia

Europe

China

Africa

India

Laos
Cambodia
Vietnam

Eritrea

Ethiopia

Indian Ocean

Australia

tic Circle

Antarctica

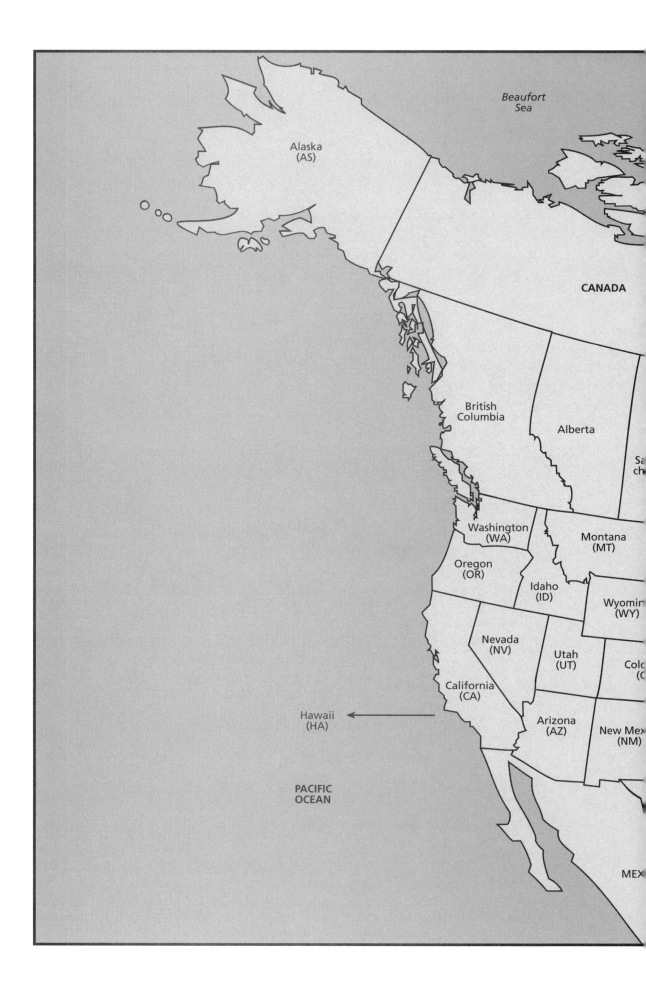

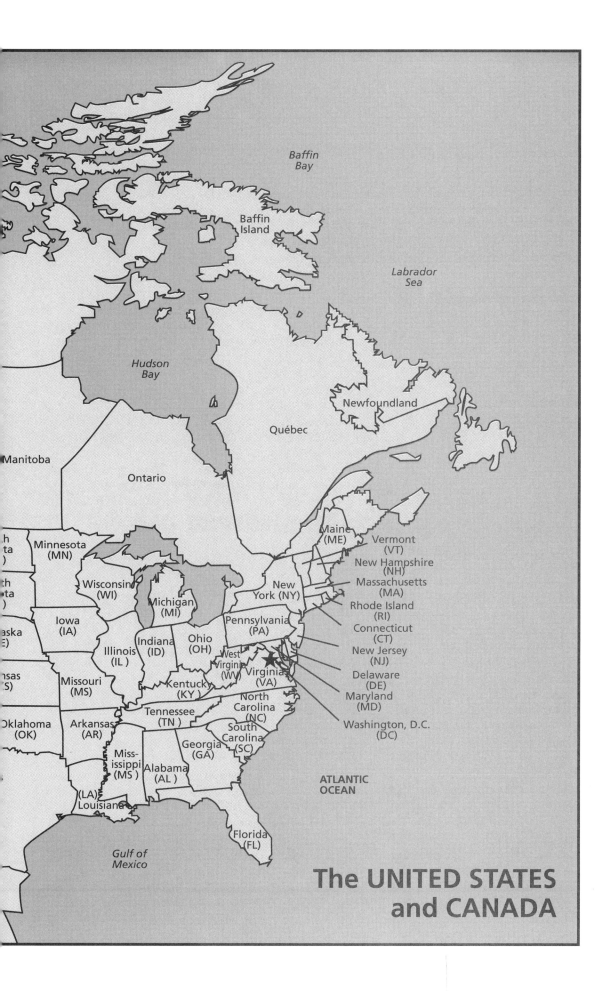

Baffin
Bay

Baffin
Island

Labrador
Sea

Hudson
Bay

Newfoundland

Québec

Manitoba

Ontario

Minnesota
(MN)

Maine
(ME)

Vermont
(VT)

New Hampshire
(NH)

Wisconsin
(WI)

Massachusetts
(MA)

Michigan
(MI)

New
York (NY)

Rhode Island
(RI)

Iowa
(IA)

Pennsylvania
(PA)

Connecticut
(CT)

Indiana
(ID)

Ohio
(OH)

New Jersey
(NJ)

Illinois
(IL)

West
Virginia
(WV)

Virginia
(VA)

Delaware
(DE)

Missouri
(MS)

Kentucky
(KY)

Maryland
(MD)

North
Carolina
(NC)

Oklahoma
(OK)

Arkansas
(AR)

Tennessee
(TN)

South
Carolina
(SC)

Washington, D.C.
(DC)

Miss-
issippi
(MS)

Georgia
(GA)

Alabama
(AL)

ATLANTIC
OCEAN

(LA)
Louisiana

Florida
(FL)

Gulf of
Mexico

The UNITED STATES
and CANADA

ABOUT THIS SERIES

Our purpose for creating this series is to provide opportunities for adult immigrants and refugees to develop English language and literacy skills while reflecting, as individuals and with others, on their changing lives.

We believe that the best adult ESL classrooms are places where learners and teachers work collaboratively, talk about issues that matter to them, use compelling materials, and engage in tasks that reflect their life experiences and concerns. We see learning as a process in which students are encouraged to participate actively and the classroom as a place where students share and reflect on their experiences and rehearse for new roles in the English-speaking world beyond its walls.

How Are the Books in the Series Organized?

Unlike most adult ESL materials, *Collaborations* is not organized around linguistic skills nor life skill competencies, but around contexts for language use in learners' lives. Each student book consists of six units, beginning with the individual and moving out through the series of ever-widening language environments shown below.

```
6   Global Community
  5   Local Community
    4   Work
      3   Home
        2 School
          1 Self
```

The units revolve around the narratives of newcomers who tell or write of their experiences. Each unit focuses on a particular site in North America, generally one that has a significant number of ESL programs and learners. In some locations, we have chosen a particular ethnic group. In others, we have made the multiethnic character of the area the focal point of the unit. It is our belief that within the marvelous diversity of newcomers, there are seeds for finding sameness—the common threads of experience as newcomers make sense of managing life in a new setting with new constraints as well as new possibilities.

Grammar, vocabulary development, language functions, and competencies are interwoven throughout the units in each student book. However, the organizing principles are reversed from most traditional materials. Rather than selecting linguistic items and then creating contexts to elicit them, *Collaborations* addresses language development and competencies as they naturally emerge from the contexts and the authentic texts. For those who wish to focus more on specific competencies or language structures, detailed indexes are provided to enable participants to identify where the item is taught, with resources for further practice in the workbook and the teacher's kit.

Collaborations is intended for use with learners of English in adult programs in school districts, community colleges, and community-based programs. While it is an excellent fit in non-credit programs, it may also be the right choice for some credit programs because of its strong emphasis on critical thinking and problem solving. The assessment component for the program—with its placement guidelines and instructions for portfolio assessment as well as more formal quizzes and tests—facilitates adaptation to either program. Particularly at the higher levels of the program, there is an emphasis on development of skills needed in academic programs, GED study, and workplace situations.

What Are the Other Components of *Collaborations*?

The supplementary **workbook** for each level is correlated to the student book. It offers independent study tasks that recycle and reinforce language points from the corresponding units of the student book. Each workbook unit has a predictable structure that contains the following:
- grammar work in context
- extended reading and writing
- vocabulary work
- competency-based tasks
- tests and self assessment

In each unit, the workbook tasks follow the sequence of the activities in the student book and further develop the unit themes.

The **teacher's resource kit** consists of a variety of materials to extend classroom activities and to facilitate and assess learners' progress. The materials listed below are provided in a format that can be inserted into the teacher's kit binder.
- the teacher's edition
- wall maps of the world and of North America
- blackline activity masters
- the assessment program
- overhead transparencies
- cassette tapes

The teacher's edition includes reduced student book pages, suggestions from the authors, insights from field test instructors who used the material in their classes, and space for teachers to keep their own teaching/learning journals. The transparencies are intended to be used for problem-posing activities, Language Experience writing, and oral language practice, among other things.

The assessment program includes traditional benchmarks such as pre-tests, individual unit checks, midterm and final exams, as well as guidelines for developing learner portfolios. The program is meant to encourage learners to set their own goals and monitor their own progress.

Finally, there are two cassette tapes for each level. The classroom tape contains all the stories from each unit of the student book as well as an authentic "review interview," for which there is an accompanying worksheet in the teacher's kit. The student tape contains all of the above with additional listening and repetition activities for use at home or in a lab.

Each unit in the student book is designed to provide at least 10 hours of activities, or 60 hours for the entire book. However, if used in conjunction with the workbook and teacher's kit, each unit provides at least 16 hours of activities for a total of 96 hours.

ABOUT THIS LEVEL

What Is Included in Each Unit?

Each unit in this level includes:

- authentic texts of some kind (photos, student writings, interview material) collected from newcomers throughout the United States and Canada;
- an opportunity to react/respond to those texts and to relate them to personal experience;
- an invitation to master the language of the text by *Playing with Story Language;*
- a task for *Listening In* in which learners have an opportunity to hear authentic and natural language from their best source of input—their teacher;
- an invitation for *Doing It in English,* in which learners practice functions of English for purposes appropriate to each context;
- a focus on *Ideas for Action,* in which learners reflect critically on their situations and what they can do to act on them;
- an opportunity for *Taking a Good Look,* in which photographs are used to stimulate discussion and thinking while developing key vocabulary;
- an opportunity for *Learning about Each Other* to foster fluency while building community among learners in the classroom;
- *Other Voices from North America* to provide expanded opportunities for reading;
- an invitation for *Looking Back,* in which learners reflect on what they have learned, what they want to study more about, and which learning activities suit them the most; and
- a *Checklist for Learning* to provide learners with a way to monitor their own progress, and to review previous material.

UNDERLYING PRINCIPLES

The language in this book is not as controlled as other materials I've used. Will this be too difficult for my students?

Adults have been learning languages, with and without language instruction, from the time of the first human migration. Students in an English-language setting acquire language most efficiently when there is something worth communicating about and when the building blocks of language are made accessible. In this scenario, acquisition becomes natural and pleasurable. The aim of this series is to provide learners with the tools they need and to create conditions in which communicating is well worth

the effort. Because language is a medium for negotiating social relationships, part of the goal is to create a classroom community in which English takes on meaning and purpose. The obstacles learners face because of their incomplete mastery of the English in the material are more than offset by compelling reasons to communicate.

What do I do if my students do not yet know the grammar or vocabulary in the stories and tasks?

Any teacher who has ever faced a class of eager ESL learners has had to grapple with the reality that learners come with differences in their prior exposure to English and with their own individual language learning timetables, strategies, and abilities. There is no syllabus which will address directly and perfectly the stage of language development of any particular learner, let alone a diverse group. This material reflects the belief that learners can benefit most when forms and functions are made available in the service of authentic communicative tasks. Teaching is most effective when it taps into areas that are ready for development.

For this reason, tasks in *Collaborations* are open-ended and multi-faceted, allowing individuals to make progress according to their current stages of development. The inclusion of numerous collaborative tasks makes it possible for more capable peers as well as instructors to provide assistance to learners as they move to new stages of growth in mastering English.

It is not necessary for learners to understand every word or grammatical structure in order to respond to a story, theme, or issue. The context created by evocative photographs, by familiar situations, and by predictable tasks usually allows learners to make good guesses about meaning even when they do not control all of the vocabulary or structures they see. Any given reading or activity is successful if it evokes a reaction in the learner, and if it creates a situation in which learners are eager to respond. When appropriate language structures and vocabulary are provided toward that end, language acquisition is facilitated. Within this framework, total mastery is not critical: total engagement is.

What do I do about errors my students make?

Errors are a natural part of the language-learning process, as learners test out their hypotheses about how the new language works. Different learners benefit from varying degrees of attention to form and function. For this reason, there are supplementary activities in the workbooks and teacher's kits where learners can give focused attention to vocabulary, grammar, functions, and competencies. The detailed indexes can also assist users in locating language forms that are of immediate concern to them. Form-focused activities can be used as material for explicit study or practice, as well as for monitoring progress in language development. This series operates on the assumption that the most important ingredient for language acquisition is the opportunity to use English to communicate about things that matter. The supplementary materials will be most effective if the time set aside to focus on form is not seen as an end in and of itself, but rather, is viewed as a necessary component in developing the tools for meaningful communication and classroom community building.

ACKNOWLEDGMENTS

This book would never have been possible without the enthusiastic help of those whose stories grace these pages. We cannot thank them all by name here, but their names appear after each story. We are grateful to colleagues, teachers, and administrators who helped so much in arranging interviews and collecting stories, among them Jean Rose, Susanna Levitt, and Bob Marseille (ABC School, Cerritos, CA); Ana Macias (El Paso Community College, TX); Nancy Gross (LaGuardia Community College, NYC); Marta Pitts (Lindsey Hopkins Technical Education Center, Miami, FL); Leann Howard and Eileen Schmitz (San Diego Community College, CA); Yom Shamash (Invergarry Learning Centre, Vancouver, BC); Adena Staben and Suzanne Liebman (College of Lake County, IL); Jenny Wittner (Chicago Commons, IL); Kit Bell (Metropolitan Skills Center, Los Angeles, CA); Harriet Lindenburg (Santa Fe Community College, NM); and Susan Joyner, Polly Scoville, and Sally Ali (Fairfax County Adult ESL Program, VA).

We thank the many fine photographers whose work is included here. While they are too numerous to name here, we would like to acknowledge those whose work appears repeatedly: Jim Higgins, whose wonderful contributions are central to the book, Ken Light, Nancy Hunter Warren, Mark Neyndorff, Ann Savino, and Sarah Hoskins.

We'd like to thank the other members of the original "think tank," Marilyn Gillespie, Jean Handscombe, and Loren McGrail, whose valuable input kicked off the project, as well as our many reviewers along the way all of whom gave shape to the final product. Our many field testers not only provided important feedback in the final stages but also allowed us to quote them extensively in the Teacher's Edition. We are thankful for their wonderful insights.

At Heinle and Heinle, Jann is grateful to Editorial Director, Roseanne Mendoza for her expert guidance not only throughout this project but also in previous projects, *Writing Workout* and *All Talk,* where her ideas on ESL materials were developed; to Erik Gunderson, for earlier encouraging the development of her ideas on teaching reading in *Reading Workout;* and to Stan Galek and Charles Heinle for believing in the project through all its ups and downs.

Gail gives special thanks to Chris Foley for the invitation to imagine aloud and to write, and to Erik Gunderson for being an invaluable part of the team when *Stories to Tell our Children* took shape and the seeds for this series were sown.

We are both grateful to Ann Keefe, assistant editor for her good nature and help with endless nitty-gritty problems; to Lisa McLaughlin, production editor, for her sensational work in producing the series and to Chris Foley for nurturing the work in its early stages. We'd also like to thank Louise Gelinas and the staff at PC&F for their fine editing and production work.

Last, but not least, the support of our families and friends is warmly appreciated. Jann would like to thank Kim for the laughter and love, John for the education in hard work and fair play, and Dolly for her exuberance and support. Gail is grateful to Z.Q. Shr for world wisdom and endlessly patient help with the computer, to Linda Lee and Jean Bernard-Johnston for their relentless support and lessons in integrity, and to Hannah Rebecca Shr, for sheer joy and perspective on what matters most.

Unit 1
Learning about Each Other in San Diego

The stories in this unit come from San Diego, California. Immigrants from all over the world live in San Diego.

San Diego, CA

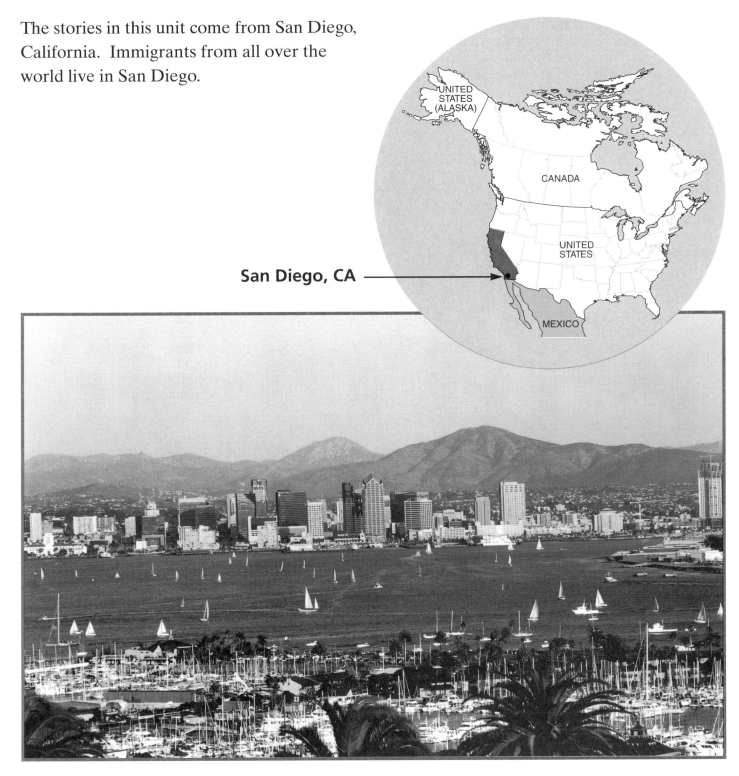

1 Stories from San Diego

These people study English at San Diego Community College.

•My name is Tsegeweini Hailemicael.
•I am from Eritrea.
•My birthdate is 4-1-52.
•I am 40 years old.
•I am married.
•I have 6 children.

•My name is Linh Dang.
•I am from Vietnam.
•My birthdate is 11-8-73.
•I am 19 years old.
•I am single
•I don't have children.

•My name is Wu Wang.
•I am from China.
•My birthdate is 7-25-25
•I am 67 years old.

• What is *your* name? Where are *you* from?

Playing with Story Language

A. Listen to each story.

B. Listen again and write the missing words.

My name ___is___ Wu Wang.

I _____ from China.

My birthdate _____ 7-25-25.

I _____ 67 years old.

Be
I **am**
You **are**
She **is**
He **is**
It **is**
We **are**
They **are**

My name _____ Linh Dang.

_____ _____ from Vietnam.

My birthdate _____ 11-8-73.

_____ _____ 19 years old.

I _____ single.

I don't _____ children.

C. Read the stories to a partner.

D. Copy Wu Wang's story. OR Cover it, listen to a partner, and write.

My name is Wu Wang.

_____

_____

_____

_____

A. Work with the class. Make a list of the countries you are from. Can you find them on the map?

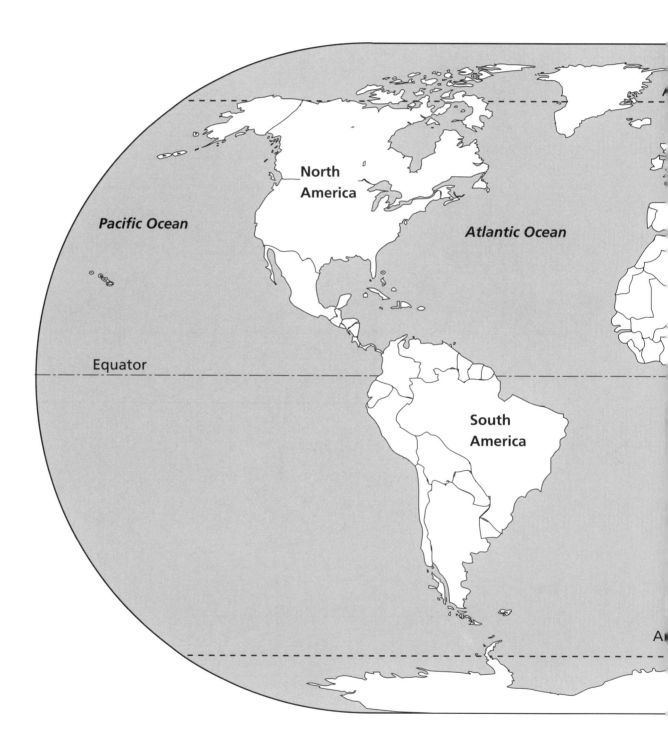

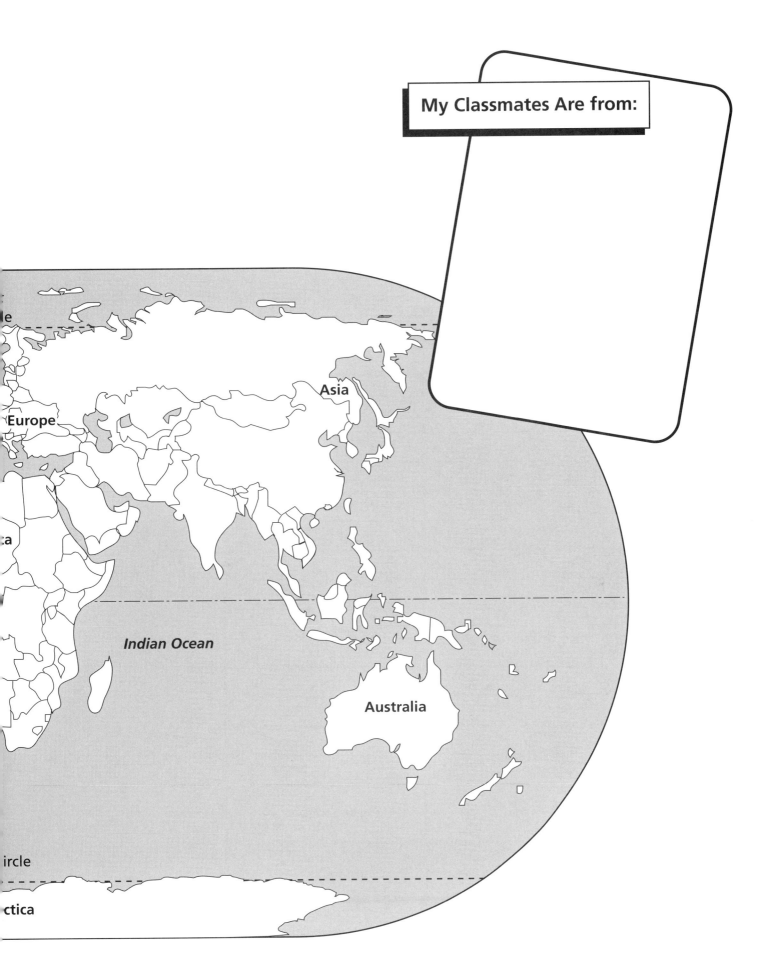

My Classmates Are from:

Asia

Europe

Indian Ocean

Australia

ircle

ctica

B. Make a class chart. Stand up and walk around the room. Ask these questions:

What's your name?
Please spell your name.
Where are you from?

What's your name, please?

Jose Gomez.

Hi, Jose. Please spell your name.

J-o-s-e G-o-m-e-z.

Thank you.

Where are you from?

Name	Country
1.	
2.	
3.	
4.	
5.	
6.	
7.	
8.	
9.	
10.	
11.	
12.	
13.	
14.	
15.	
16.	
17.	
18.	
19.	
20.	

C. Look at the map on pages 4 and 5 again. Write the names of your classmates next to their countries.

D. What countries are you and your classmates from? Share with each other some information about your countries.
Your teacher will write your information on the board. Copy it.

Country	A Little Bit of Information
USA	It has 50 states. It is in North America.
Canada	It has 10 provinces and 2 territories. It is in North America.

Taking a Good Look: Places in the World

A. Do any of these pictures look like your country? Tell a partner.

B. With the class, label some of the things you see in the pictures such as *lake, palm tree,* and *mosque.*

1

2

3

4

5

6

7

8

 Bringing the Outside in: Pictures of Your Country

Bring pictures of your country to class. Put the pictures on the wall.
Write the name of the country under each picture.

6 Listening in: Your Teacher's Personal Information

Listen to your teacher. Fill in the chart. Ask questions if you wish.

My Teacher

Name	
City, State, and Country	
Marital Status (single or married?)	
Children	
Other Personal Information	

7 Doing It in English: Asking Personal Questions

 Work with a partner. Fill in the chart. Ask these questions.

What's your name? (Please spell that.)
Where are you from?
Are you single or married?
Do you have children?

Ask any other questions you have, too.

My Partner

Name	
City and Country	
Marital Status (single or married?)	
Children	
Other Personal Information (phone number, favorite food, or anything else!)	

8 More Stories from San Diego

A. Listen to Eileen Schmitz's story.
Circle new words.
Can you guess the meaning of
some of them?

Eileen Schmitz is the teacher
of the San Diego students.

1

I like to make silhouettes of my
students. We use the light from the
overhead projector. We put black
paper on the wall, and students stand
against it.

2

I draw their heads with a pencil. I
can do it very fast, in five seconds.

3

We cut out the silhouettes. We put
them on the wall, and we write our
names and countries underneath.
Then we have a big book on the wall!

B. This is the story of the San Diego class. How is the class similar to your class?

There is / there are	
There is **There are**	one student from Cambodia. two students from China.

Our Class

There are eighteen people in our class. There is one woman from Cambodia and one woman from Vietnam. There are two men from China. There are five people from Russia and one person from Eritrea. There are four students from Mexico and four from Guatemala. Eight of us are married, and the rest of us are single!

Singular and Plural	
Singular (1)	Plural (2+)
student teacher story class	students teachers stor**ies** class**es**
man woman person child	**men** **women** **people** **children**

With your class, write your class story on the board. (Look at p. 6 for help). Copy the story into your notebook.

Doing It in English: Telling What You Like to Do

Eileen Schmitz likes to make silhouettes. What do you like to do?
Tell the class. Ask your teacher.

The Picture Dictionary may help.

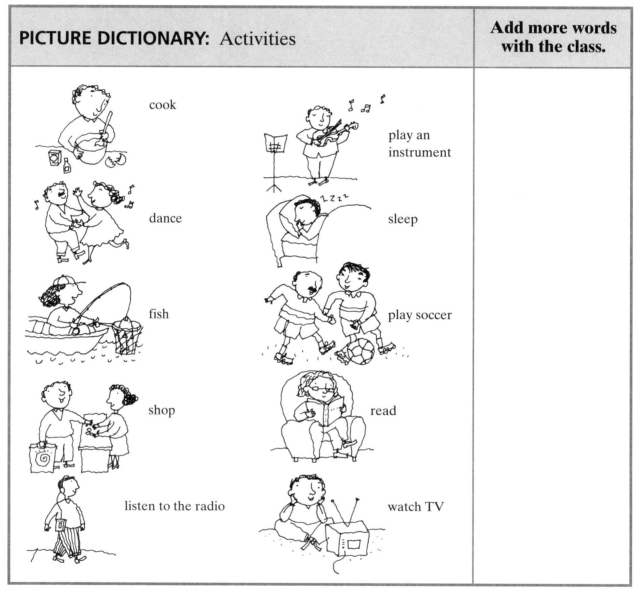

PICTURE DICTIONARY: Activities	Add more words with the class.
cook	
dance	
fish	
shop	
listen to the radio	
play an instrument	
sleep	
play soccer	
read	
watch TV	

Write a sentence.

I like _____ and _____, but

I don't like _____.

10

Other Voices from North America

 Read the two stories.
Are they similar in any way?
Tell a partner.

WORDS I WANT TO REMEMBER

I am from Vietnam. It's a small country in Asia. It is beautiful. There are many lakes and rivers and rice. I miss it. I am homesick. Please help my country because it is poor. Thank you!

Phuong Viet Duo studies English in the Fairfax County Adult Education Program in Virginia.

I am from Moscow. It is the biggest city in Russia. The winters are cold and long, but the summers are beautiful. In summer I miss it. I always miss my friends.

Tamara Berman studies English in the ABE/ESL program at the University of New Mexico at Los Alamos.

11 Ideas for Action:

Coping with Homesickness

Phuong Viet misses his country. He is homesick. What can he do?

Talk about this in English or your native language. Write some suggestions with the class.

1. *He can make new friends in his class.* _____

2. _____

3. _____

4. _____

12 Looking Back

Think about your learning. Fill in the blanks.
Then tell the class your ideas.

A. In this unit I learned _____

_____.

B. I want to study more about _____.

C. The activity I liked best was 1   2   3   4   5   6   7   8   9   10   11

because _____.

D. The activity I liked least was 1   2   3   4   5   6   7   8   9   10   11

because _____.

Checklist for Learning

I. **Vocabulary:** Check (✔) the words you know. Add more words if you wish.

Places on the Map	**Things People Like to Do**
_____ China	_____ play soccer
_____ Vietnam	_____ watch TV
_____ South America	_____ play Ping-Pong
_____ North America	_____ shop
_____ Asia	_____ fish
_____ Africa	_____ listen to the radio
_____ Pacific Ocean	_____ sleep
_____ Atlantic Ocean	_____ ski
_____ Russia	_____ cook
_____ Cambodia	_____ dance
_____ Mexico	_____ read
_____ Guatemala	_____ play an instrument
_____ Eritrea	_____ _____
_____ _____	_____ _____

II. **Language:** Check (✔) what you can do in English. Add more ideas if you wish.

I can

_____ read stories.　　　　　　　　_____ tell what I like to do.

_____ tell about my country.　　　 _____ _____

_____ ask my classmates ques-　　_____ _____
tions about themselves.

_____ ask my teacher to repeat
something.

III. **Listening:** Listen to the Review Interview at the end of Unit 1. Ask your
teacher for a *Collaborations* worksheet.

Unit 2

Helping Each Other Learn in Chicago

The stories in this unit come from the Chicago area. Chicago attracts newcomers from all over the world, especially Mexico, Poland, India, the Philippines, and the former Soviet Union.

UNITED STATES (ALASKA)

CANADA

UNITED STATES

MEXICO

Chicago, IL

Alicia Silva's Story

I like to read and listen. I like to do everything in this class. But I'm nervous because I don't speak. I need more help.

Alicia Silva is from Puerto Rico. She is on the right in the photo. She studies at the Chicago Commons.

- When are you nervous in class?
- When are you relaxed in class?

2 Playing with Story Language

A. Listen to the story.

B. Listen again and write the missing words.

listen
speak
do
read
need

I like to _____*read*_____ and _____.

I like to _____ everything in this class.

But I'm nervous because I don't _____.

I _____ more help.

C. Read the story to a partner.

D. Copy the story. OR Cover the story, listen to a partner, and write.

I like to read and listen.

_____

_____

_____

_____

_____

_____

... 21

3 Doing It in English: Telling How You Like to Learn

Tell how you like to learn in class. Check (✔) **YES** or **NO.**

In this class, I like to

	YES	NO
speak.	❑	❑
listen.	❑	❑
speak my language.	❑	❑
read stories.	❑	❑
write at the board.	❑	❑
stay in my seat.	❑	❑
laugh.	❑	❑
work alone.	❑	❑
work with a partner.	❑	❑
work with a group.	❑	❑
(other) _____	❑	❑

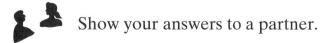 Show your answers to a partner.

What does your teacher want you
to do in class? Listen and check (✔).
Ask questions when you do not understand.

Excuse me?

Will you repeat that?

Words to Tell *How Often*		
always		100%
often		
sometimes		
never		0%

In this class, the teacher wants you to

	ALWAYS	OFTEN	SOMETIMES	NEVER
speak English	❏	❏	❏	❏
speak your language	❏	❏	❏	❏
be relaxed	❏	❏	❏	❏
laugh	❏	❏	❏	❏
write on the board	❏	❏	❏	❏
listen to your classmates	❏	❏	❏	❏
work alone	❏	❏	❏	❏
work with a partner	❏	❏	❏	❏
work with a group	❏	❏	❏	❏

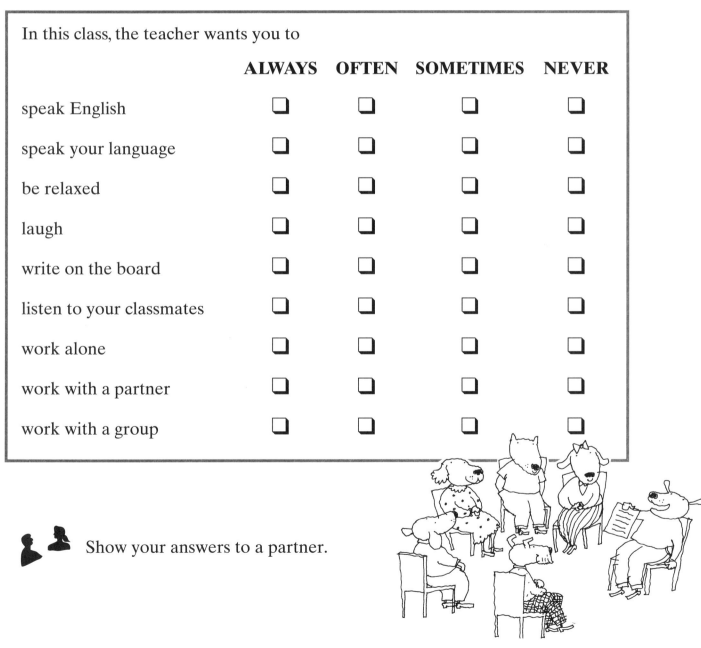

Show your answers to a partner.

5 Taking a Good Look: Ways to Learn

A. Who is reading? _____5_____   Who is listening? _____

      Who is writing? _____   Who is speaking? _____

B. Who is nervous? _____   Who is relaxed? _____

C. Which picture looks most like your class? _____

1

2

6 Learning about Each Other: Our Learning Styles

Interview a partner. Ask these questions:

When are you nervous in class?

When are you relaxed?

Write the answers.

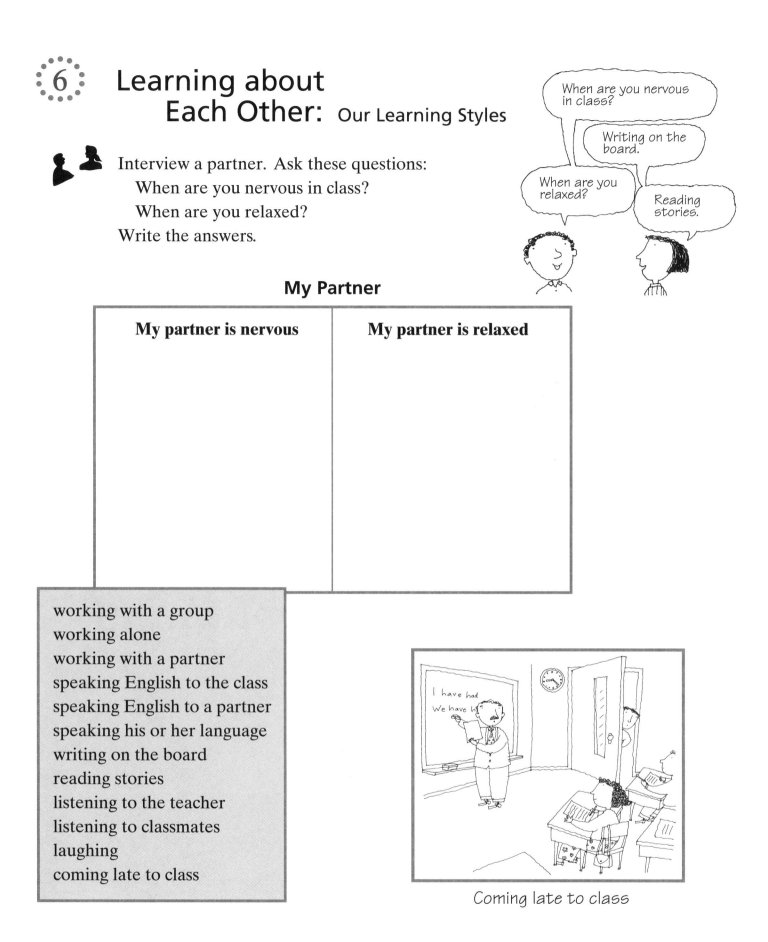

My Partner

My partner is nervous	My partner is relaxed

working with a group
working alone
working with a partner
speaking English to the class
speaking English to a partner
speaking his or her language
writing on the board
reading stories
listening to the teacher
listening to classmates
laughing
coming late to class

Coming late to class

Tell the class about your partner.

Doing It in English: Labeling Things in the Classroom

This is an ESL class in Chicago. Label some things in the classroom.
The Picture Dictionary below might help.

screen

Now label things in *your* classroom.

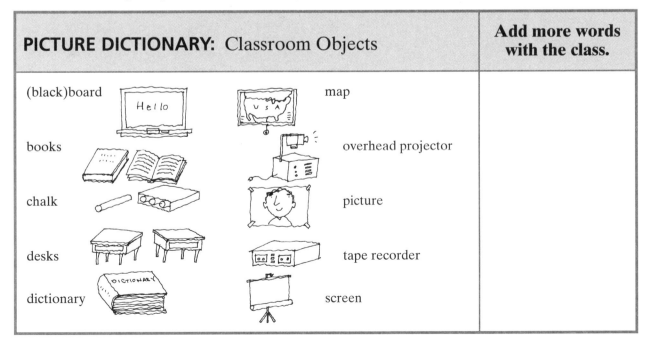

PICTURE DICTIONARY: Classroom Objects	**Add more words with the class.**
(black)board	map
books	overhead projector
chalk	picture
desks	tape recorder
dictionary	screen

More Stories from Chicago

Read the two stories about learning. How do Adam and
Gladys feel? Are they like you?

When I came to the U.S., I was alone. But in my
English class, we work together. I have a lot of
friends. It really changed my life.

Adam Czerw is from Poland. He studies English in Chicago with
his friends. Adam is the third person from the right in the photo.

It makes a difference when the classroom is full of students. Then you are not alone. There are so many nationalities in our class! There are so many different accents! It is fun to listen to them. It is fun to talk to people from all over the world.

Gladys Soto is second from the right in the photo. She is from Puerto Rico and studies ESL at the Chicago Commons.

 Circle new words in the stories. Talk to a partner about the new words. Then read one story aloud to your partner.

 9 # Bringing the Outside in: Things That Help You Learn

Bring to class something that helps you learn English: a book, a magazine, a dictionary, flash cards, a game, or a cassette tape. Show the class.

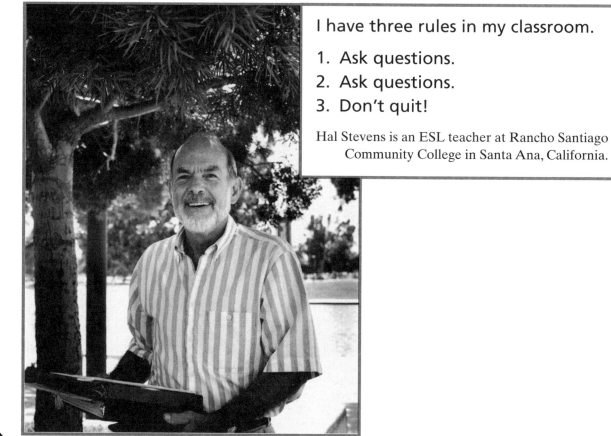

I have three rules in my classroom.

1. Ask questions.
2. Ask questions.
3. Don't quit!

Hal Stevens is an ESL teacher at Rancho Santiago Community College in Santa Ana, California.

 Do you agree with Hal Steven's rules for his classroom? Do you like to ask questions?

What questions can you ask when you need help? Write some questions with your class. Practice them.

Can you pronounce that?

What does "rule" mean?

How can you help your classmates learn English? How can they help you?

Ask for your classmates' phone numbers. Make a class list.*

Name	Phone Number
1.	
2.	
3.	
4.	
5.	
6.	
7.	
8.	
9.	
10.	
11.	
12.	
13.	
14.	
15.	
16.	
17.	
18.	
19.	
20.	

*If you don't want to share your number, you can say, "I'd rather not say."

Other Voices from North America

Choose **one** story to read.
Is the writer similar to you?
Tell a partner.

In America I can learn in school, no matter how old I am. Some of my classmates are young people, and some are older than me. We all help each other learn.

Chan Wong So San studies English at LaGuardia Community College in New York City. She is from China.

IDIOMS
no matter
be in a hurry

WORDS I WANT TO REMEMBER

It is hard for me to learn English. I have small children. I do not have a babysitter, and I cannot always come to class.

Vera Vlasenko studies ESL at Greenfield Community College in Northampton, Massachusetts. She is from Russia.

I am in a hurry to learn English. School helps me a lot. But out of class, it is hard to practice English. Almost all people in Miami speak Spanish.

Miguel Hernandez is from Colombia. He studies English at Lindsey Hopkins Technical Education Center in Miami, Florida.

 13

Looking Back

Think about your learning. Fill in the blanks.
Then tell the class your ideas.

A. In this unit I learned _____

_____ .

B. I want to study more about _____ .

C. The activity I liked best was 1 2 3 4 5 6 7 8 9 10 11 12

because _____ .

D. The activity I liked least was 1 2 3 4 5 6 7 8 9 10 11 12

because _____ .

Checklist for Learning

I. Vocabulary: Check (✔) the words you know. Add more words if you wish.

Classroom Words

_____ map
_____ desk
_____ chalk
_____ dictionary
_____ picture
_____ tape recorder
_____ screen
_____ (black)board
_____ books
_____ overhead projector
_____ _____
_____ _____

Verbs

_____ speak
_____ listen
_____ read
_____ write
_____ work alone
_____ work with a partner
_____ work with a group
_____ laugh
_____ _____
_____ _____
_____ _____
_____ _____

II. Language: Check (✔) what you can do in English. Add more ideas if you wish.

I can

_____ read short stories.
_____ tell how I like to learn.
_____ understand my teacher's classroom instructions.
_____ name many things in the classroom.
_____ ask questions when I don't understand.
_____ understand phone numbers.
_____ _____
_____ _____

III. Listening: Listen to the Review Interview at the end of Unit 2. Ask your teacher for a *Collaborations* worksheet.

No **Place**
Like **Home:** Stories from Massachusetts

The stories in this unit come from Massachusetts. Many immigrants from Southeast Asia (Cambodia, Laos, and Vietnam) live there.

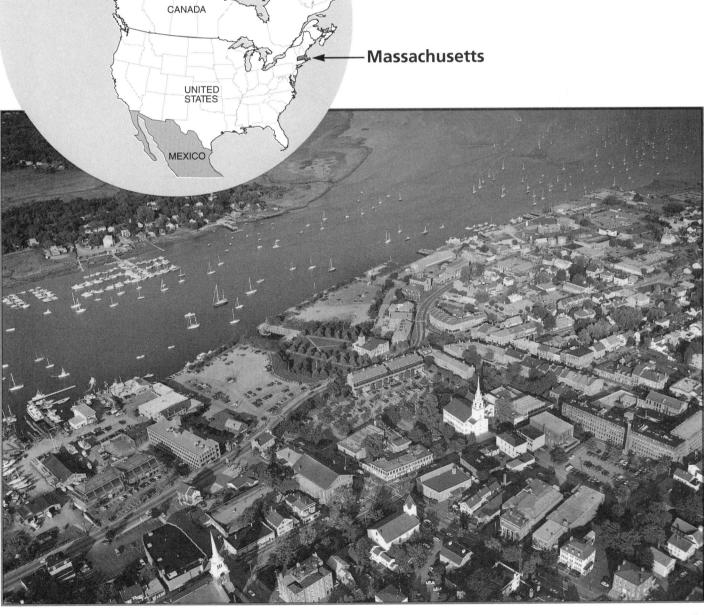

← Massachusetts

Narin Sao's Story

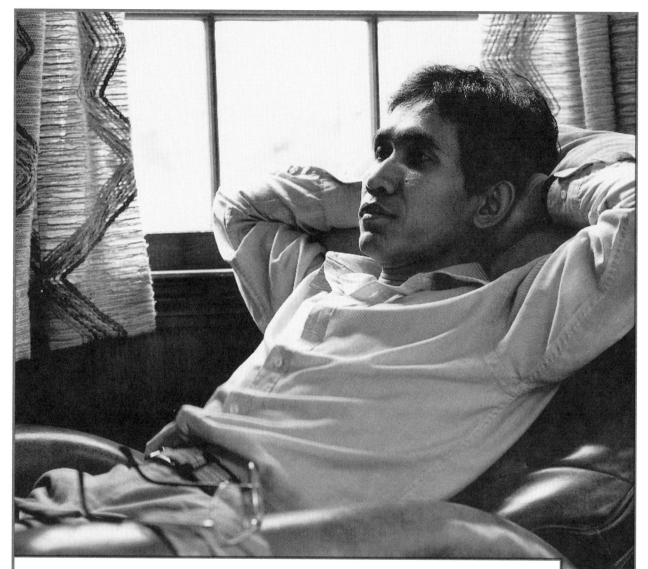

Every night I listen to songs from my country. In my mind I see my grandparents' farm. I walk in fields of coconut and orange trees. I eat fresh pineapple. There's no place like home.

Narin Sao lives in Lowell, Massachusetts. He is from Cambodia.

• Close your eyes. Think of home.

• What do you see? Draw it or write some words to describe it.

2 Playing with Story Language

A. Listen to the story.

B. Listen again and write.

---

1. Every night I listen to _____*songs from my country*_____.

 my   country   from   songs

2. In my mind _____.

 farm   I   see   my   grandparents'

3. I walk in fields of _____.

 orange   and   coconut   trees

4. I _____.

 fresh   pineapple   eat

5. There's _____.

 like   home   no   place

C. Read the story to a partner.

D. Copy the story. OR Cover it, listen to a partner, and write.

 Every night I listen to songs from my country.

_____

_____

_____

_____

_____

Doing It in English: Telling about Your Family

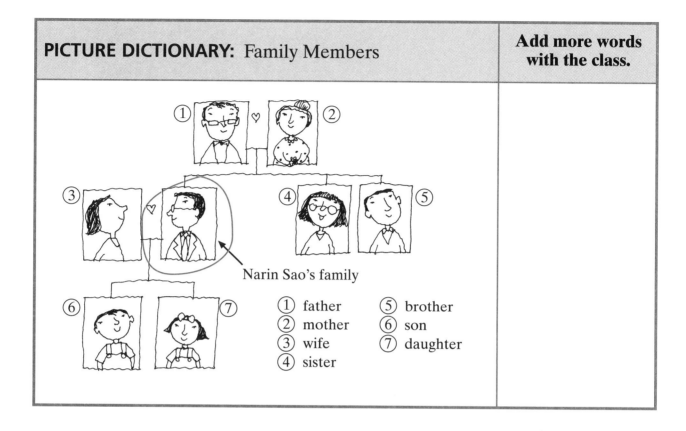

PICTURE DICTIONARY: Family Members	Add more words with the class.

Narin Sao's family

① father   ⑤ brother
② mother   ⑥ son
③ wife   ⑦ daughter
④ sister

Fill in the chart. Write about your family members.

Name	Relationship (father, mother, sister,. . .)	Where Do They Live? (city and country)

Tell a partner about your family.
Who lives far away? Who lives near? Who lives in your house?

4 Listening in: Your Teacher's Family

Listen to your teacher talk about his or her family. Fill in the chart.
Ask to see photographs!

When you don't understand, you can say:

Please spell it.

Excuse me?

I don't understand.

My Teacher's Family

Relationship	Name	Where Do They Live?

 Tell a partner what you understood.

5 Bringing the Outside in: Family Photos

 Bring in photos of your family. Ask and answer questions with a partner.

In and On with Place Names		
in +	city state country	on +	avenue street road

Who's that?

My sister.

Where does she live?

In Haiti.

Taking a Good Look: Family Relationships

A. Can you find these people?

mother

father

brother

sister

husband

wife

daughter

son

grandmother

grandchild

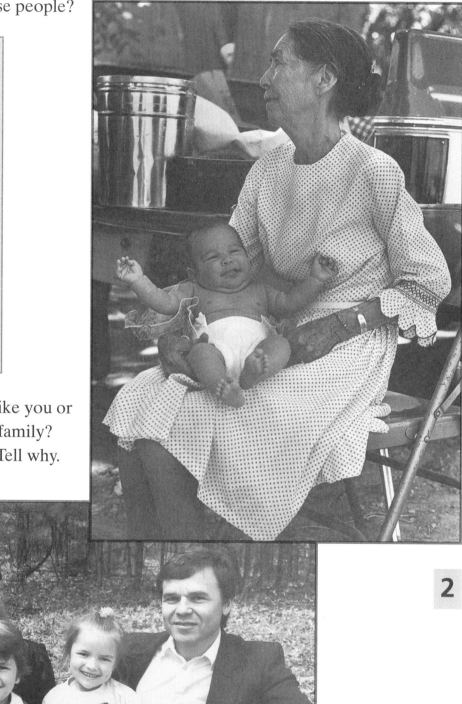

B. Which person is like you or someone in your family? Show a partner. Tell why.

1

2

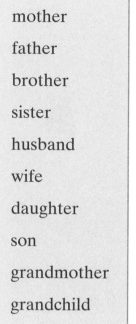

3

4

7 Learning about Each Other: Where Our Families Live

Find out about your partner's family. Fill in the chart.

MY PARTNER'S FAMILY (Partner's name _____)

Family Member's Name	Where Does He or She Live?

8 Doing It in English: Comparing Lives

A. Read Peter Baraban's story. Are you like him? How?

I have lived in America for one year and four months. I grew up in the former Soviet Union. I'm always thinking about my country because it is my homeland. Almost all my family—my parents, brothers, and sisters—are there. I want them to come here.

Peter Baraban lives in Greenfield, Massachusetts. He studies English at Greenfield Community College.

B. What about You?

Circle **YES** or **NO**.

I have lived in America for more than one year.	**YES**	**NO**
I have lived in America for less than one year.	**YES**	**NO**
I'm always thinking about my country.	**YES**	**NO**
My family is there.	**YES**	**NO**
My family is here.	**YES**	**NO**
I want my family to come here.	**YES**	**NO**

C. Copy your **YES** sentences below. Add more if you wish.

_____

_____

_____

_____

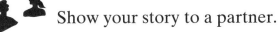 Show your story to a partner.

9 More Stories from Massachusetts

Read the two stories about new homes. How do the stories make you feel? Tell the class.

In Laos, grandparents spend their time at home in their yards. The yard is a vegetable garden for the family. But here I have no yard. I live on the third floor in an apartment building. There is a parking lot below.

This grandmother lives in Lowell, Massachusetts. She is from Laos.

I bought a house. Now we can welcome everyone here. My father's friends live here too. We all live together. We welcome everybody. It's a Cambodian custom.

Heng Bun Chea lives in Lowell, Massachusetts. He comes from Cambodia. He is on the far right in the photo.

 Circle new words in the stories. Talk to a partner about the new words. Then read one of your stories aloud to your partner.

10 Other Voices from North America

Choose **one** story to read.
Is the writer similar to you?
Tell a partner.

WORDS I WANT TO REMEMBER

I live in Washington, DC. Last summer I went home to Uzbekistan. I saw my mother. I visited all my friends. When can I go home again? I don't know. I spent all my money.

Leonid Bodkin is from Uzbekistan.

My name is Keren Wu. I live in Amherst with my husband. I have a daughter in China.

My daughter's name is Shi Liang. She is six years old. She's a beautiful girl. She is learning to write Chinese. She can write a letter to me. I love her so much and I miss her very much.

Keren Wu studies at Greenfield Community College in Greenfield, Massachusetts.

11 Ideas for Action: Staying in Touch

Think about your family and friends far away.
How are you going to stay in touch?

I Am Going to Write a Letter to (My)	I Am Going to Call (My)	I Am Going to Visit (My)

 Tell a partner.

> **IDIOM**
> stay in touch

12 Looking Back

Think about your learning. Fill in the blanks.
Then tell the class your ideas.

> **A.** In this unit I learned _____
>
> _____ .
>
> **B.** I want to study more about _____ .
>
> **C.** The activity I liked best was 1   2   3   4   5   6   7   8   9   10   11
>
> because _____ .
>
> **D.** The activity I liked least was 1   2   3   4   5   6   7   8   9   10   11
>
> because _____ .

Checklist for Learning

I. Vocabulary: Check (✔) the words you know. Add more words if you wish.

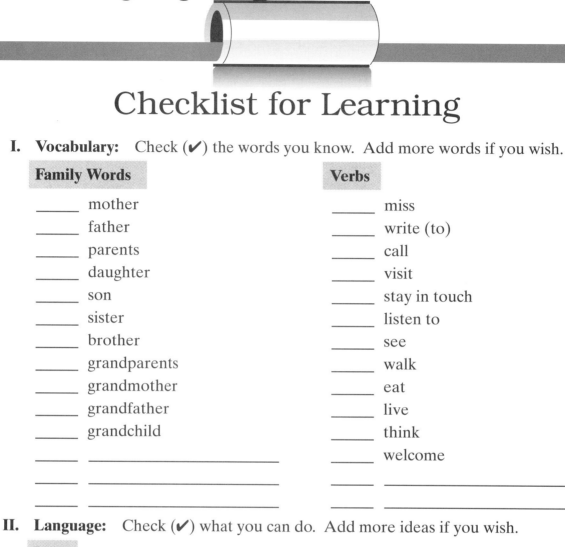

Family Words

_____ mother
_____ father
_____ parents
_____ daughter
_____ son
_____ sister
_____ brother
_____ grandparents
_____ grandmother
_____ grandfather
_____ grandchild
_____ _____
_____ _____
_____ _____

Verbs

_____ miss
_____ write (to)
_____ call
_____ visit
_____ stay in touch
_____ listen to
_____ see
_____ walk
_____ eat
_____ live
_____ think
_____ welcome
_____ _____
_____ _____

II. Language: Check (✔) what you can do. Add more ideas if you wish.

I can

_____ read short stories.
_____ talk about my home.
_____ tell where my family lives.
_____ understand my teacher when she tells about her family.
_____ say, "Please repeat that," when I don't understand.
_____ say, "Excuse me?" when I don't understand.
_____ ask questions about a partner's family.
_____ _____
_____ _____

III. Listening: Listen to the Review Interview at the end of Unit 3. Ask your teacher for a *Collaborations* worksheet.

Unit 4 **Working Hard** in the Southwest

Southwestern United States

The stories in this unit come from the Southwest. Many Mexicans and Mexican Americans live in the southwestern states of Texas, New Mexico, and Arizona.

Ramon Ramirez's Story

I start work at 5:00 in the morning. For breakfast, I cook steak, eggs, bacon, and pancakes. I work from 5:00 A.M. to 1:30 P.M. Sometimes I work from 5:00 A.M. to 5:00 P.M.! I'm a morning person. I have to be!

Ramon Ramirez is from Mexico. He is a restaurant chef in New Mexico. He studies English at Santa Fe Community College.

IDIOM
a morning person

- Is your day like Ramon's day?

- Do you work hard, too?

Telling Time	
at	5:00 A.M.
at	12:00 P.M.
from	5:00 A.M. *to* 1:30 P.M.
from	5:00 A.M. *to* 5:00 P.M.

2 Playing with Story Language

A. Listen to the story.

B. Listen again and write the missing words.

> work
> make
> at
> and
> I'm
> from
> to

I start work _____ 5:00 in the morning. I

_____ steak, eggs, bacon, _____

pancakes. I work _____ 5:00 A.M.

_____ 1:30 P.M. Sometimes I _____

from 5:00 A.M. to 5:00 P.M. _____ a morning person.

I have to be!

C. Read the story to a partner.

D. Copy the story. OR Cover it, listen to a partner, and write.

I start work at 5:00 in the morning.

_____

_____

_____

_____

_____

_____

_____

3 Doing It in English: Telling about Your Day

Write about your day.

Copy the sentences in the **Activities** box.

Add more sentences if you wish.

At five o'clock in the morning (5:00 A.M.), Ramon starts work.

At one-thirty in the afternoon (1:30 P.M.), Ramon finishes work.

My Day

Time

A.M.	6:00
	6:30
	7:00
	7:30
	8:00
	8:30
	9:00
	9:30
	10:00
	10:30
	11:00
	11:30
	12:00
P.M.	12:30
	1:00
	1:30
	2:00
	2:30
	3:00
	3:30
	4:00
	4:30
	5:00
	5:30
	6:00
	6:30
	7:00
	7:30
	8:00
	8:30
	9:00
	9:30
	10:00
	10:30
	11:00
	11:30
	12:00

Activities

I get up.
I start work.
I finish work.*
I go to school.
I eat dinner.
I go to bed.

*Remember: Work can be housework or schoolwork, too!

 Show your "day" to a partner.

Listening in: Your Teacher's Day

Listen to your teacher tell about his or her day. Copy the sentences next to the correct times.

When you don't understand, you can say:

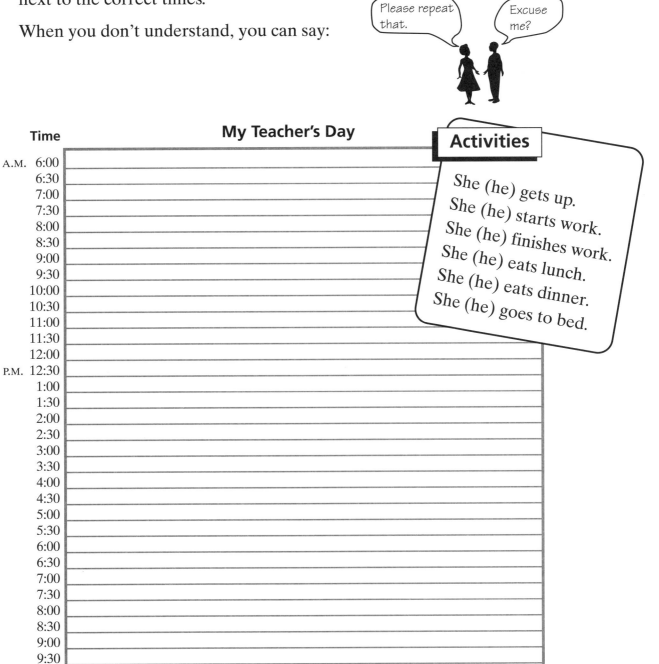

Please repeat that.

Excuse me?

Activities

She (he) gets up.
She (he) starts work.
She (he) finishes work.
She (he) eats lunch.
She (he) eats dinner.
She (he) goes to bed.

Time	My Teacher's Day
A.M. 6:00	
6:30	
7:00	
7:30	
8:00	
8:30	
9:00	
9:30	
10:00	
10:30	
11:00	
11:30	
12:00	
P.M. 12:30	
1:00	
1:30	
2:00	
2:30	
3:00	
3:30	
4:00	
4:30	
5:00	
5:30	
6:00	
6:30	
7:00	
7:30	
8:00	
8:30	
9:00	
9:30	
10:00	
10:30	
11:00	
11:30	
12:00	

Simple Present

I You We They	**go** to bed.	She He	**goes** to bed.

Taking a Good Look: Work

Talk with the class.

A. Where do these people work?
What jobs do they do?

B. Who works hard?

C. Which job do you like?
Which job is similar to your job?

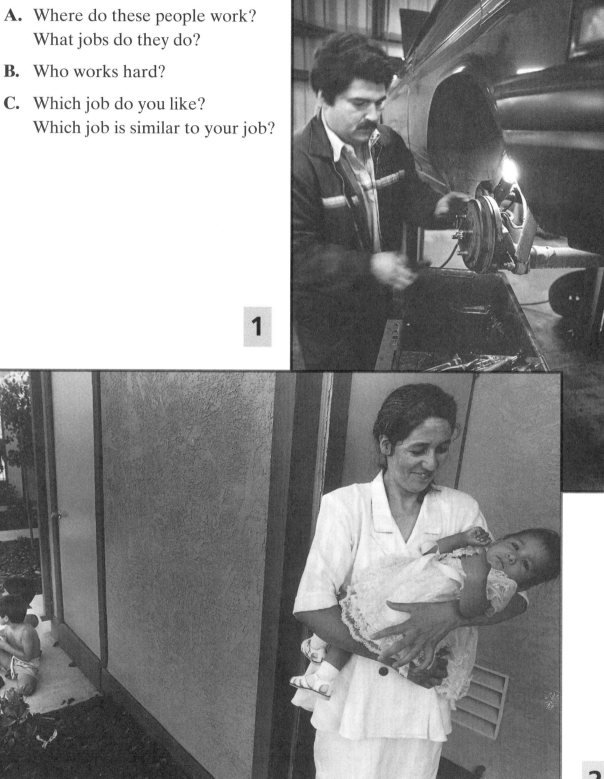

1

2

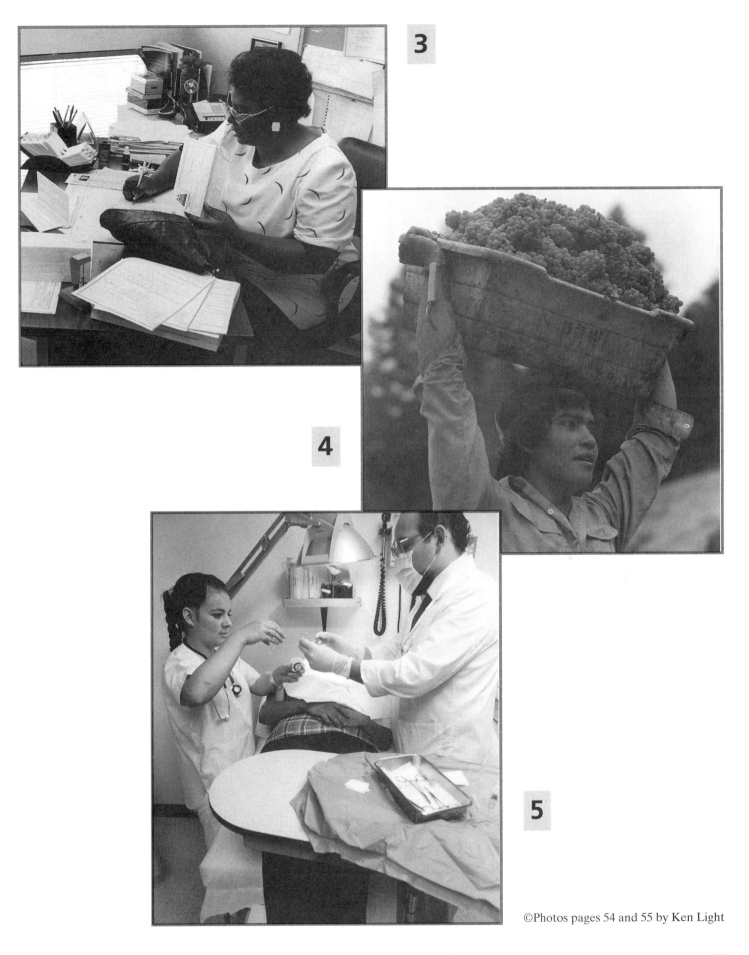

3

4

5

Learning about
Each Other: Our Daily Schedules

Walk around the room. Ask each classmate
the four questions in the chart below.
Fill in the chart.

Name	When do you get up?	When do you start work?	When do you finish work?	When do you go to bed?

Tell the class:

    Who gets up early?
    Who gets up late?
    Who works hard?
    Who goes to bed late?

7 Doing It in English: Comparing Lives

A. Read Khampoo's story. Is your life similar to his? How?

> I leave my first job at 2:00 P.M. I pick up my son from school. When my wife gets home at 4:00, I go to my second job. Sometimes I work overtime on Saturday. On Sunday we go to the supermarket.
>
> Khampoo and his family live in Lowell, Massachusetts. They are from Laos.

B. What about You?

Circle **YES** or **NO**.

I have one job.	**YES**	**NO**
I have two jobs.	**YES**	**NO**
I work on Saturday.	**YES**	**NO**
I stay home on Saturday.	**YES**	**NO**
On Sunday I go to the supermarket.	**YES**	**NO**
On Sunday I relax.	**YES**	**NO**
I work hard.	**YES**	**NO**

Days of the Week

Sunday
Monday
Tuesday
Wednesday
Thursday
Friday
Saturday

C. Copy your **YES** sentences below. Add more sentences if you wish.

_____

_____

_____

_____

 Show your story to a partner.

8 More Stories from the Southwest

Read the two stories about working hard. Is your work similar to Maria's or Victoria's?

Tell a partner or the class.

We start work at 8:30. Usually, we finish at 5:00. We clean the same rooms every day. Today we worked real fast. English class starts at 4:30. If we want to come to English class, we have to finish all our rooms early. We have to work harder.

Maria Fernandez is from Mexico. She works at a hotel and studies English at Santa Fe Community College in New Mexico.

I like my job. But I work a lot overtime. I don't have time to be with my children. I am very tired after work. I would like to change my job. I want to use my brain more than my body.

Victoria Cease is from Mexico. She works and studies English at Levi Strauss in El Paso, Texas.

IDIOM
work overtime

Circle new words in the stories. Talk to a partner about the new words. Then read one story aloud to your partner.

9 Other Voices from North America

Choose *one* story to read.
How is the writer similar to you?

Tell a partner.

IDIOM
spend time

UNITED STATES (ALASKA)

British Columbia

CANADA

UNITED STATES

New York

MEXICO

I sew at a factory in Chinatown, in New York City. Every day I work more than ten hours. Sometimes I work seven days a week. I am very tired after work. I don't like this job. I get little money, but I spend a lot of time.

Huan Ying Li studies English at
LaGuardia Community College in New York.

Every morning I take my children to school. I come back home and take my wife to school. Then I go to school too. I do not have a job. I came to Canada only six months ago. In the evening, my family studies English together. Life is very hard and expensive in Canada. I must learn English quickly to find a job.

Naseer Al Janabi is from Jordan. He studies ESL at Invergarry
Learning Centre in Vancouver, British Columbia.

WORDS I WANT TO REMEMBER

Bringing the Outside in: Samples of Our Work

What work can you do? Bring something to class.

For example, if you knit, bring in a sweater.

If you cook, bring in some food.

If you paint, bring in a painting.

Tell the class what you can do.

I can cook tortillas!

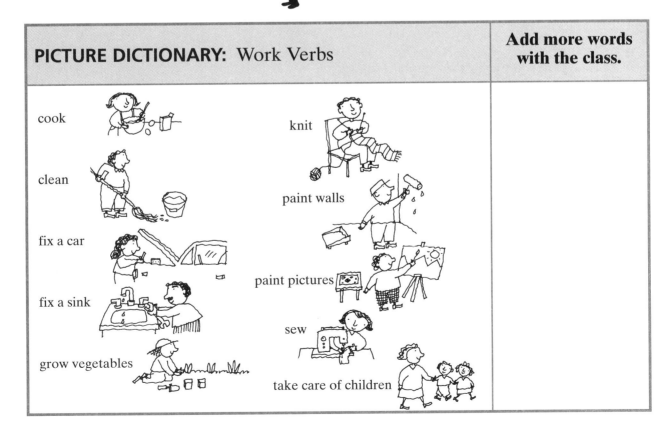

PICTURE DICTIONARY: Work Verbs	Add more words with the class.
cook	
clean	
fix a car	
fix a sink	
grow vegetables	
knit	
paint walls	
paint pictures	
sew	
take care of children	

11 Ideas for Action: Managing Busy Lives

Is your work hard? Are you sometimes tired? What can you change in your life? Check (✔) your answer.

	YES	NO
I can relax more at work.	❏	❏
I can relax more in English class.	❏	❏
I can work shorter hours.	❏	❏
I can ask my children to help at home.	❏	❏
I can cook faster meals at home.	❏	❏
I can share childcare with friends, neighbors, or classmates.	❏	❏
I can eat better.	❏	❏
I can listen to music at night or take a walk.	❏	❏
(other) _____	❏	❏

 Tell a partner.

12 Looking Back

Think about your learning. Fill in the blanks.
Then tell the class your ideas.

> **A.** In this unit I learned _____
>
> _____.
>
> **B.** I want to study more about _____.
>
> **C.** The activity I liked best was 1   2   3   4   5   6   7   8   9   10   11
>
> because _____.
>
> **D.** The activity I liked least was 1   2   3   4   5   6   7   8   9   10   11
>
> because _____.

Checklist for Learning

I. Vocabulary: Check (✔) the words you know. Add more words if you wish.

Verbs

_____ get up
_____ go to bed
_____ start
_____ finish
_____ eat
_____ work overtime
_____ sew
_____ clean
_____ fix a car
_____ knit
_____ paint
_____ grow vegetables
_____ take care of children
_____ relax
_____ _____

Workplaces

_____ hospital
_____ field
_____ factory
_____ office
_____ home
_____ school
_____ restaurant
_____ hotel
_____ _____
_____ _____
_____ _____
_____ _____
_____ _____
_____ _____

II. Language: Check (✔) what you can do in English. Add more ideas if you wish.

I can

_____ read short stories.
_____ talk about time.
_____ tell about my daily activities.
_____ understand my teacher when she tells about her day.
_____ say, "Please repeat that," when I don't understand.
_____ say, "Excuse me?" when I don't understand.
_____ ask questions about people's daily activities.
_____ say the days of the week.
_____ _____

III. Listening: Listen to the Review Interview at the end of Unit 4. Ask your teacher for a *Collaborations* worksheet.

Unit 5

Familiar Faces and Places in Miami

The stories in this unit come from Miami, Florida—a very international city. More than 60% of its population are foreign born. This unit focuses on Little Havana, a section of Miami where many Cuban immigrants live.

Miami, FL

Avelino Gonzalez's Story

In this photo, I am shopping at the Calle Ocho market in Little Havana.

In Little Havana in Miami, I can find everything from my country—Cuban coffee, mangoes, papayas, and pineapples. I can find my people too. It feels like home!

Avelino Gonzalez studied ESL at Lindsey Hopkins Technical Education Center in Miami. Now he is a law student at the University of Miami. He comes from Cuba.

- Does your neighborhood feel like home?

- What can you find? Who can you find?

2 Playing with Story Language

A. Listen to the story.

B. Listen again and write.

> In Miami, I can _____ everything from my country
>
> in Little Havana—Cuban _____, mangoes, papayas,
>
> _____ pineapples. I can find my _____
>
> too. It feels like _____!

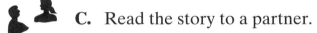

C. Read the story to a partner.

D. Copy the story. OR Cover it, listen to a partner, and write.

In Miami, I can _____

_____

_____

_____

_____

3 Doing It in English: Telling What You Like

Look at the Picture Dictionary.

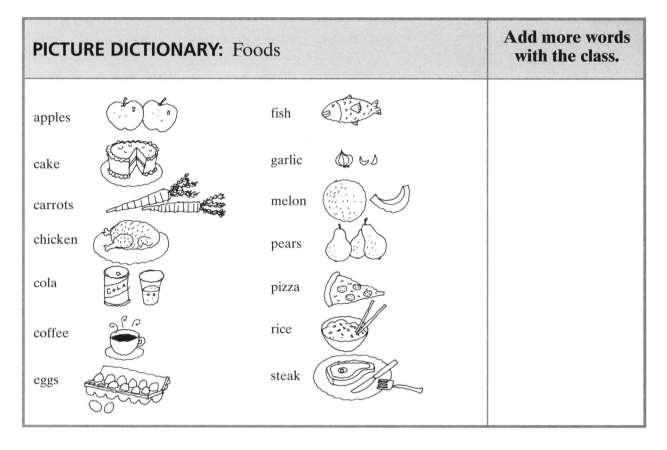

PICTURE DICTIONARY: Foods		Add more words with the class.
apples	fish	
cake	garlic	
carrots	melon	
chicken	pears	
cola	pizza	
coffee	rice	
eggs	steak	

Write the foods you like and don't like.

I Like	I Don't Like

I don't like American coffee. It's like water! I prefer Cuban coffee. It's strong and sweet.

Tell a partner or the class what you like and don't like. Also, tell the class where you like to shop for food.

4 Listening in: Your Teacher's Favorite Foods

Listen as your teacher explains what he or she likes to eat. Circle
the foods he or she likes. Put an **X** over foods he or she doesn't like.

She likes fish, rice, carrots....

She does't like pizza or coffee.

Tell a partner what you understood.

5 Bringing the Outside in: Comparison Shopping

With the class, choose one food item (a pound of carrots, a dozen
large eggs, etc.). Before the next class, find out the price of the item
at your local market. Tell the class or write the prices on the board.
Are the prices the same?

Saying Prices	
59¢	= fifty-nine cents
$1.20	= one twenty *or* one dollar and twenty cents
$4.99	= four ninety-nine *or* four dollars and ninety-nine cents

6 Taking a Good Look: Neighborhood Places

A. These are places in Little Havana. Do you have these places in your neighborhood too? Tell a partner.

B. Which places are important to you? What do you do there? Tell the class.

> There are both a bank and a park in my neighborhood.

> There's no bank in my neighborhood.

5

6

8

7

Doing It in English: Following Directions

This is a map of Avelino Gonzalez's neighborhood.

Listen to your teacher. See where your teacher leads you.
Follow the map with your finger. Start from Avelino's house.

Listen for these words and phrases:

turn right ⌐→   go straight ——→

turn left ←⌐   go 1 (2, 3) blocks

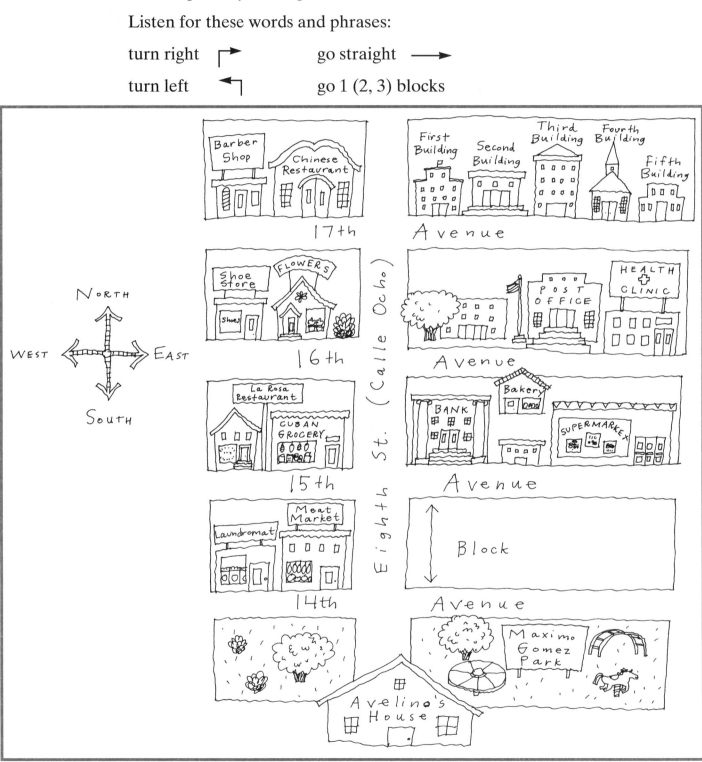

Learning about Each Other: Our Neighborhoods

 Draw a map of your neighborhood. Write the important places. Then show your map to a partner. Tell about your neighborhood and the places you go.

> Here is my bank. It's nearby.
> Here is the supermarket. It's far.

Veronika Argueda is from Nicaragua. She studies English at Plaza Resolana in Santa Fe, New Mexico.

EXTRA WORK: With the class, talk about the good and bad things in your neighborhood.

More Stories from Miami

Read more about Avelino and his community. Which story do you like best? Why?

How do people in your community help each other?

Here, I am watching a game of dominoes in Maximo Gomez Park in Little Havana.

In our community, the men come here to talk and play dominoes. Their wives stay at home.

These men help each other. The men who speak English help the men who don't. The English speakers have a special role in the community.

Present Continuous	
I **am** You **are** She **is** He **is** We **are** They **are**	**watching** a game.
Use **present continuous** to tell about activities happening now, at the moment of speaking.	

Here my grandmother is sitting in front of her house.

I came here in 1992, and my grandmother helped me a lot. I lived in her house in Little Havana for a year, but she didn't take money for food or rent.

Connecting Sentences

You can connect two sentences like this:
. . . . ., **and** . . . . . .
. . . . ., **but** . . . . . .

Circle new words in the stories. Talk to a partner about the new words. Then read one story aloud to your partner.

10 Other Voices from North America

Choose **one** story to read.
Is the writer similar to you?

Tell a partner.

WORDS I WANT TO REMEMBER

I live in Arlington, Virginia. My neighbor on the left is from the U.S. On the right is a Latin American. In the front is an Ethiopian.

My neighbors from the U.S. are not friendly. I don't know them. We only say "hi" when we bump into each other in the elevator or on the street. Nobody has time to talk. Everybody is busy.

Berhane Admasu is from Ethiopia. She studies ESL at the Willston Center in Fairfax County, Virginia.

I know my neighbors very well. I live in an international community. One person is from Germany. One is from Peru. One is American.

Each year we have a party. They like my spicy Indian food. Sometimes, we give each other rides. When somebody goes on vacation, we watch the house. We get the mail and water the plants. We always help each other.

Ila Desai is from India. She studies ESL at the Herdun Center in Fairfax County, Virginia.

IDIOM
bump into

Ideas for Action: Meeting People in Your Community

These men meet at Maximo Gomez Park in Little Havana. They play dominoes and talk. They make new friends.

Where do people in your community meet and talk? How do people in your community make new friends? Share ideas with the class.

Places People Meet

_____

_____

_____

Ways to Make New Friends

_____

_____

_____

Looking Back

Think about your learning. Fill in the blanks.
Then tell the class your ideas.

A. In this unit I learned _____.

B. I want to study more about _____.

C. The activity I liked best was   1   2   3   4   5   6   7   8   9   10   11

because _____.

D. The activity I liked least was   1   2   3   4   5   6   7   8   9   10   11

because _____.

13 Learning Log

Checklist for Learning

I. Vocabulary: Check (✔) the words you know. Add more words if you wish.

<table>
<tr><td>Foods and Drinks</td><td>Places in the Community</td></tr>
<tr><td>_____ apples</td><td>_____ market</td></tr>
<tr><td>_____ steak</td><td>_____ supermarket</td></tr>
<tr><td>_____ rice</td><td>_____ bank</td></tr>
<tr><td>_____ fish</td><td>_____ shoe store</td></tr>
<tr><td>_____ eggs</td><td>_____ post office</td></tr>
<tr><td>_____ cola</td><td>_____ park</td></tr>
<tr><td>_____ chicken</td><td>_____ community center</td></tr>
<tr><td>_____ garlic</td><td>_____ health center</td></tr>
<tr><td>_____ pineapple</td><td>_____ laundromat</td></tr>
<tr><td>_____ carrots</td><td>_____ _____</td></tr>
<tr><td>_____ pizza</td><td>_____ _____</td></tr>
<tr><td>_____ _____</td><td>_____ _____</td></tr>
</table>

<table>
<tr><td>Verbs</td><td>_____ play</td></tr>
<tr><td>_____ go straight</td><td>_____ help</td></tr>
<tr><td>_____ turn right</td><td>_____ watch</td></tr>
<tr><td>_____ turn left</td><td>_____ _____</td></tr>
<tr><td>_____ find</td><td>_____ _____</td></tr>
</table>

II. Language: Check (✔) what you can do in English. Add more ideas if you wish.

I can

_____ read short stories.   _____ tell the price of something.

_____ tell what foods I like   _____ understand directions.
and don't like.   _____ name places in my community.

_____ understand my teacher   _____ _____
when he tells what he likes.   _____ _____

III. Listening: Listen to the Review Interview at the end of Unit 5. Ask your
teacher for a *Collaborations* worksheet.

Unit 6

Celebrating Together in Cerritos, California

The stories in this unit come from ABC School in Cerritos, California. Cerritos has immigrants from all over the world, and ABC School teaches English to 2,000 of them every year!

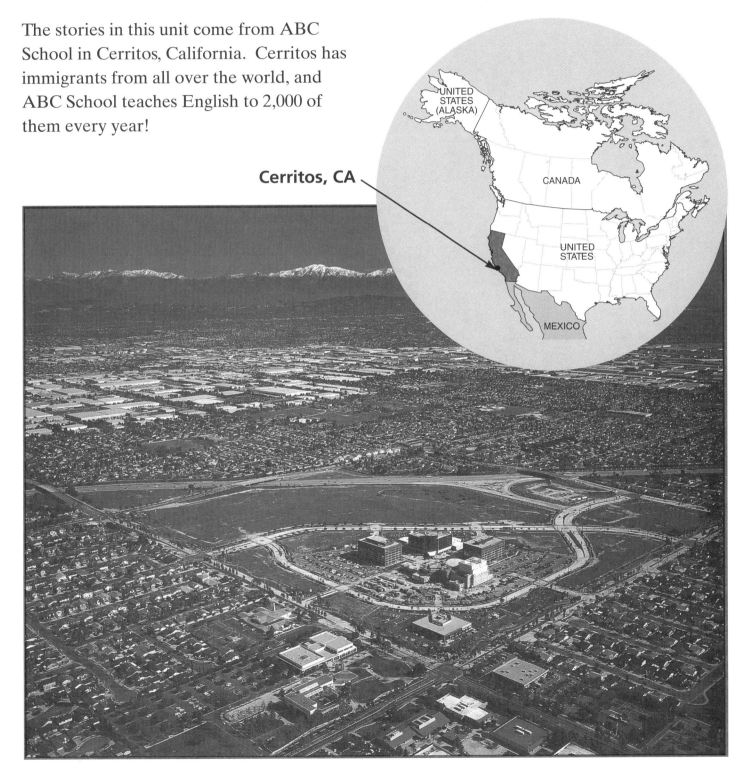

Cerritos, CA

Susanna Levitt's Story

Our school had a celebration at the end of the year. Students from each country decorated a room to teach about their country. One Mexican woman taught us a Mexican dance. An older Indian man played the flute. Some Japanese students showed beautiful old kimonos. In this picture, Lesli is teaching about the Chinese language.

After this day, we all looked at each other with new eyes!

Susanna Levitt, Teacher
ABC School

- How do you celebrate?

- How do others celebrate?

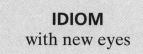

IDIOM
with new eyes

2 Playing with Story Language

A. Listen to the story.

B. Listen again and write the missing words.

1. Our school ___had a celebration at___ the end of the year.
   celebration   had   a   at

2. Students from each country _____ to teach
   about their country.   room   a   decorated

3. One Mexican _____ a Mexican dance.
        us   taught   woman

4. An older _____ the flute.
        man   Indian   played

5. Some Japanese _____ kimonos.
        showed   beautiful   students   old

6. In this picture, Lesli _____ the Chinese language.
        about   is   teaching

7. After this day, we all looked at each other with new eyes!

C. Read the story to a partner.

D. Copy three sentences from the story. OR Cover it, listen to a partner, and write.

Our school had a celebration

_____

_____

_____

Doing It in English: Telling about a Celebration

Think about a holiday or celebration you had here or in your country. What did you do? Put a check (✔).

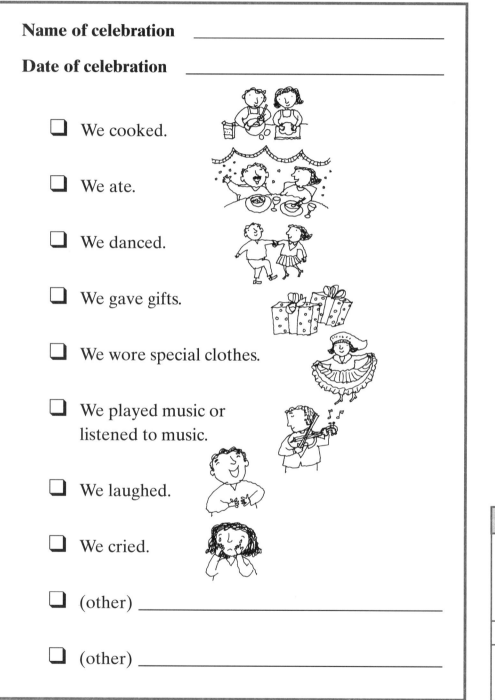

Name of celebration _____

Date of celebration _____

❏ We cooked.

❏ We ate.

❏ We danced.

❏ We gave gifts.

❏ We wore special clothes.

❏ We played music or listened to music.

❏ We laughed.

❏ We cried.

❏ (other) _____

❏ (other) _____

Simple Past	
Present	**Past**
cook	cook**ed**
dance	danc**ed**
visit	visit**ed**
laugh	laugh**ed**
cry	cr**ied**
eat	**ate**
wear	**wore**
give	**gave**

Tell about your celebration.
Show your answers to a partner.

④ Listening In: Your Teacher's Celebration

Listen to your teacher talk about a recent celebration.
What did your teacher do? Put a check (✔).

Name of celebration _____

Date of celebration _____

❏ He or she cooked.

❏ He or she ate.

❏ He or she danced.

❏ He or she gave gifts.

❏ He or she wore special clothes.

❏ He or she played music
or listened to music.

❏ He or she laughed.

❏ He or she cried.

❏ Other _____

❏ Other _____

  What did you learn about your teacher? Tell a partner.

⑤ Bringing the Outside in: Things We Use in Celebrations

Bring a picture or photo of a celebration.

Or bring something you use, eat, or wear
in a celebration.

Tell your class about it.

What's this?

It's a piñata.

How do you use it?

You hit it with
a stick . . .

6 Doing It in English: Planning a Celebration

You have learned a lot of English. It's time to celebrate!

A. With your class, plan your celebration.
Circle **YES** or **NO**. Add new ideas.

Who are we going to invite?

Our families	**YES**	**NO**
Our neighbors	**YES**	**NO**
Other students	**YES**	**NO**

_____

_____

_____

What are we going to eat?

Food from our homelands	**YES**	**NO**
Drinks	**YES**	**NO**

    soda
    juice
    coffee
    tea

_____

_____

What are we going to do?

perform songs and dances	**YES**	**NO**
teach songs and dances	**YES**	**NO**
listen to music	**YES**	**NO**
wear special clothes	**YES**	**NO**

_____

_____

What are we going to bring?

tape recorder	**YES**	**NO**
guitar	**YES**	**NO**
other instruments	**YES**	**NO**
paper plates, napkins	**YES**	**NO**

_____

_____

B. Work in a small group. Think about what you are going to do. Are you going to show something? Are you going to teach something? Are you going to cook something? Fill in the chart.

Name	What are you going to bring, cook, or do?

What did your group decide? Tell the class.

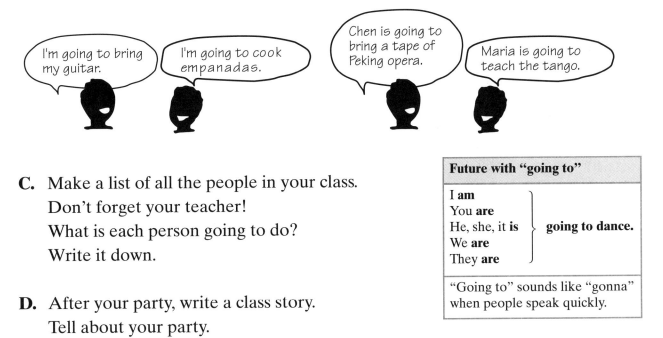

I'm going to bring my guitar.

I'm going to cook empanadas.

Chen is going to bring a tape of Peking opera.

Maria is going to teach the tango.

C. Make a list of all the people in your class. Don't forget your teacher! What is each person going to do? Write it down.

D. After your party, write a class story. Tell about your party.

Future with "going to"	
I **am** You **are** He, she, it **is** We **are** They **are**	going to dance.
"Going to" sounds like "gonna" when people speak quickly.	

Taking a Good Look: Celebrations and Traditions

What is the celebration?
Where do you think it is?
Is it like a celebration in your native country?

1

2

3

4

5

6

Learning about Each Other: Our Holidays

A. What holidays do you celebrate here? Tell a partner.
The Picture Dictionary may help.

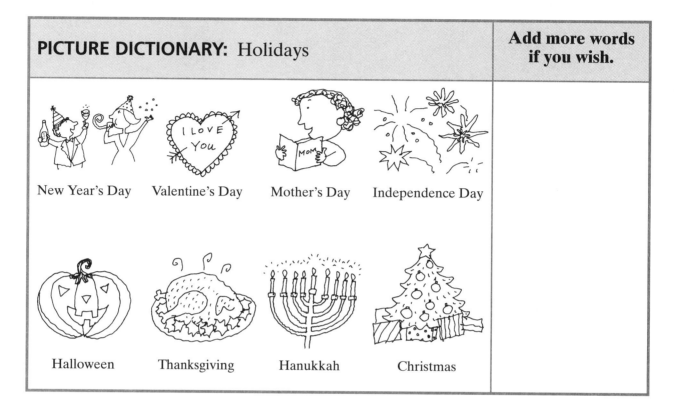

PICTURE DICTIONARY: Holidays	Add more words if you wish.
New Year's Day Valentine's Day Mother's Day Independence Day	
Halloween Thanksgiving Hanukkah Christmas	

B. Which of these holidays do you celebrate in your
native country? Put a check (✔).

C. What are other important holidays in your
native country? Write three.

_____

_____

_____

D. Talk with a partner about your favorite holidays.

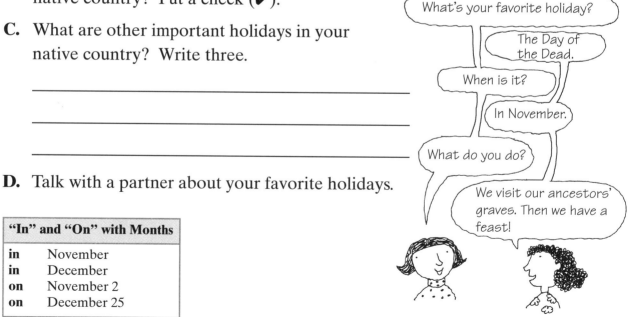

What's your favorite holiday?

The Day of the Dead.

When is it?

In November.

What do you do?

We visit our ancestors' graves. Then we have a feast!

"In" and "On" with Months	
in	November
in	December
on	November 2
on	December 25

Doing It in English: Marking the Calendar

 A. Work with a small group. Write the names of holidays here or in your native countries.

1 **January**	2 **February**	3 **March**	4 **April**
	14-Valentine's Day ♡		
5 **May**	6 **June**	7 **July**	8 **August**
9 **September**	10 **October**	11 **November**	12 **December**

B. Make a big calendar with your class. Which holidays come from another country? Mark them with a star.

C. Mark the four seasons on the calendar. Are these the same as the seasons in your country? Now write your favorite holiday for each season.

Winter _____ Spring _____

Summer _____ Fall _____

Show a partner. Are any of your favorite holidays the same?

The students at ABC School in Cerritos talked about their celebration. Read the two stories. Which story do you like best? Which photo do you like best? How do you like to celebrate?

At our party, we danced beautiful Mexican dances. The Mexican students wore typical hats and clothing. I saw clothes from all the states of Mexico. One man sang romantic songs. The mariachis played beautiful music. It made me feel proud to be Mexican!

Elizabeth Zertuche is from Mexico. She studies English at ABC School, Cerritos, California.

For our celebration, we wanted more than just an exhibit. We wanted some activities. It's more fun! Weddings are very important for Chinese people. So we showed how to do a wedding. The bride and groom bow to God, bow to the parents, and then to each other. Then they go to the love nest!

Jenny Chao is a student at ABC School, Cerritos, California. She is from China.

IDIOM
love nest

 Circle new words in the stories. Talk to a partner about the new words. Then read one story aloud to your partner.

11 Other Voices from North America

Choose **one** story to read.
Does it make you remember something?
Tell a partner.

WORDS I WANT TO REMEMBER

Our New Year is called Tet. I must prepare all this food. I give it to my Creator, to my family ancestors, and to my children and grandchildren. They must come to visit me. They must wish me a happy long life.

Mrs. Nguyen is from Vietnam. Now she lives in Lowell, Massachusetts.

Ramadan is a great month for Muslims. We do not eat from sunrise to sunset during Ramadan. This teaches us to think about people who are hungry or homeless. We pray to God many times. Every night we cook rice, meat, chicken, soup, salad, and dessert. The Muslim law is, if you are angry with someone, you should go to him and apologize. You should let go of all the bad things you did. You should stop hating people.

Mohammed Mehrzad (left) is from Afghanistan. Yahya Arisheh (right) is from Jordan. They study ESL at Invergarry Learning Centre in Vancouver, British Columbia, Canada.

12 Ideas for Action: Keeping Traditions

My daughter doesn't remember China. For the Moon Festival, I took her to Los Angeles. We celebrated with other Chinese. I don't want her to forget this custom.

Z.Q. Shr lives in San Francisco, California. He is from China.

Which celebrations will you keep? Which ones will you change?
Make two lists. Share your ideas with the class.

Celebrations I Will Keep

_____

_____

_____

Celebrations I Will Stop or Change

_____

_____

_____

13 Looking Back

Think about your learning. Fill in the blanks.
Then tell the class your ideas.

> **A.** In this unit I learned _____
>
> _____.
>
> **B.** I want to study more about _____.
>
> **C.** The activity I liked best was 1 2 3 4 5 6 7 8 9 10 11 12
>
> because _____.
>
> **D.** The activity I liked least was 1 2 3 4 5 6 7 8 9 10 11 12
>
> because _____.

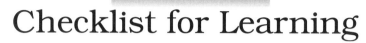

Checklist for Learning

I. Vocabulary: Check (✔) the words you know. Add more words if you wish.

Verbs: Past Tense	**Holidays**
_____ cooked	_____ New Year's Day
_____ ate	_____ Valentine's Day
_____ danced	_____ Mother's Day
_____ gave	_____ Independence Day
_____ wore	_____ Halloween
_____ played	_____ Thanksgiving
_____ laughed	_____ Hanukkah
_____ cried	_____ Christmas
_____ _____	_____ _____
_____ _____	_____ _____
_____ _____	_____ _____

II. Language: Check (✔) what you can do in English. Add more ideas if you wish.

I can

_____ read short stories.

_____ tell about my celebrations or holidays.

_____ understand my teacher's story about celebrations or holidays.

_____ tell about celebrations in other countries.

_____ say and read the months of the year.

_____ make a calendar of special events.

_____ plan a great party!

_____ _____

III. Listening: Listen to the Review Interview at the end of Unit 6. Ask your teacher for a *Collaborations* worksheet.

APPENDIX • • •

NUMBERS

1	one
2	two
3	three
4	four
5	five
6	six
7	seven
8	eight
9	nine
10	ten

11	eleven
12	twelve
13	thirteen
14	fourteen
15	fifteen
16	sixteen
17	seventeen
18	eighteen
19	nineteen

20	twenty
21	twenty-one
22	twenty-two
23	twenty-three
24	twenty-four
25	twenty-five
26	twenty-six
27	twenty-seven
28	twenty-eight
29	twenty-nine

30	thirty
31	thirty-one

40	forty
50	fifty
60	sixty
70	seventy
80	eighty
90	ninety
100	one hundred

INDEX ...